MICAH BROOKS

ALL THINGS NEW EP
Songbook

"The title, All Things New, is taken from the main line in the bridge of *Here Comes The Lord*. Revelation 21:5 says, "Behold, I am making all things new!" When Jesus comes back, He will be making all things new again. As Christians, it's our greatest hope. Making things new means that we have reunion with loved ones that we've lost. It means that the darkest parts of us aren't hidden inside any longer because they don't need to exist there. Most importantly, it means that we have perfect closeness to Jesus who's the author and the perfecter of our faith. We can't wait for all things to be made new!"

MICAH BROOKS COMPANY

www.micahbrooks.com

Micah Brooks

Produced by Micah Brooks
Recorded, Mixed, and Mastered
at WorshipHeart Studios

Josh Harvill: Drums
Dylan Rosson: Electric Guitars
Chris Perdue: Cello
Micah Brooks: Lead & Backing Vocals,
Bass, Piano, Keys, Guitars, Mandolin,
Banjo, Loops, and a Shaker

Published by WorshipHeart Publishing

Cover Design by Micah Brooks Kennedy

Also available for the All Things New EP:
CDs
MP3s
Backing Tracks
Individual Lead Sheets
Individual Chord Charts

For booking and touring information visit micahbrooks.com

All To Your Name (4:13)
(Micah Brooks/Corey Voss)
Saved (4:37)
(Micah Brooks/Kirk Kirkland)
Jesus My Savior (4:11)
(Micah Brooks/Jason Dyba)
Here Comes The Lord (3:47)
(Micah Brooks/Jared Anderson)
Heal The Brokenhearted (4:16)
(Micah Brooks/Tony Wood)
Love Has Overcome (4:12)
(Micah Brooks/Shelly E. Johnson)

All To Your Name (4:13)

(Micah Brooks/Corey Voss)

All To Your Name is the first song on the All Things New EP. I am privileged to have co-written this song with Corey Voss. Corey is a talented worship leader from the Nashville area.

We met together to write an upbeat worship song. One that would invite the congregation to lift their hands from the beginning of a service. I believe that we do not need to be warmed up or wait for a slower song later in the service to raise our hands in worship. In Psalms 132 we are commanded to lift our hands before God. It's an act of total surrender. There are few places in life where we need to lift our hands in this way. God gives us this place of doing when worshipping him. It's remarkably unique!

I remember speaking with Corey about how we wanted the verses to use the old hymn-themed pattern. Notice at the end of verse two we speak about Jesus coming back again. These are awesome words from the book of Revelation when Jesus rides in with His eyes like fire and breath like wind. His every word is faithful and true. I love the power of that imagery. This is Jesus Whom we worship. He is not dead, He is fully alive and coming back as a conquering King!

The bridge invites every saint to raise their hands before the Lord. This is a type of the great rehearsal here on earth. The power of learning how to worship God in this life must yield dividends in our eternal home.

May you always have this great hope inside and never bury it or want to hide it. Let your life be lived all to the name and glory of Jesus Christ Who was and is and is to come. Amen!

All To Your Name

Lead Sheet
BPM = 114

Micah Brooks Kennedy
and Corey Voss

PAGE 2 - All To Your Name
BRIDGE
CHORUS
TAG
G
CMaj9
Dsus
CMaj9/E
D/F♯
Dsus/F♯
Em7
C
N.C.
Gsus
wor - ship. Now — All the saints, all hands raised, ev - 'ry praise, all to
Your name. Je - sus Christ glo - ri - fied. Ev - 'ry praise, all to Your name. All the Your name.
I raise my hands up to the sky to praise the name of Je - sus Christ, the
One who taught my heart to rise in wor - ship. I give my life to mag - ni - fy all
to Your name, Lord Je - sus Christ, who was and is and is to come, I wor - ship.
Who was and is and is to come, I wor - ship. Who was and is and
is to come, I wor - ship.

Saved (4:37)

(Micah Brooks/Kirk Kirkland)

Romans 10:9 says, "If you believe in your heart and confess with your mouth that Jesus is Lord, raising Him from the dead, you will be saved." From what I know, this is the only way to find eternal salvation. Our days under the sun are numbered, but our days with God are not.

I wrote the song *Saved* with songwriter and singer, Kirk Kirkland. We spoke about the importance of the verse in Romans above. We wanted to use that line as part of the chorus to be sung over and over.

Beyond believing in your heart and speaking with your mouth, it's critical to recognize the power of Jesus' blood shed on the cross. Scripture says that we were bought by the blood of Jesus. There was an eternal transaction made on your behalf. It is in the power of that shed blood that your sins are forever forgiven.

Equally as important as understanding the work of Jesus on the cross for my sins is that my salvation must be worked out with fear and trembling. It is my responsibility to live each day as if my salvation could be lost. While I do not believe it can be snatched up by Satan's hand for any single action, I certainly believe I should live my life in reverent fear of the God who made the universe. He wants to know us and he has given us standards by which to live. It is through obedience that we display our love for our creator.

May you rejoice with the words of your mouth and the belief in your heart that you are saved by the God who made the universe yet still knows the number of hairs on your head.

Saved
Lead Sheet
BPM = 130
Micah Brooks Kennedy
and Kirk Kirkland
INTRO
CHORUS
B
I de - clare with my mouth that
Je-sus is Lord, be - lieve in my heart He's ris - en and I'm saved! I'm
TURNAROUND
saved!
Guitar Lead Line
Bsus
B/D♯
E
VERSE
C♯m7
F♯
1. With my heart I do be - lieve,
2. Share the joy of this good news.
G♯m7
with my mouth I must con - fess
Our be - lief is with - out shame.
Je - sus' blood
Je - sus died

PAGE 2 - Saved

CHORUS

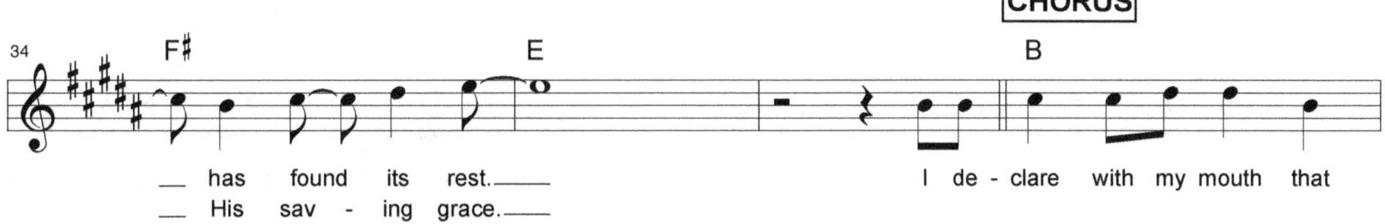

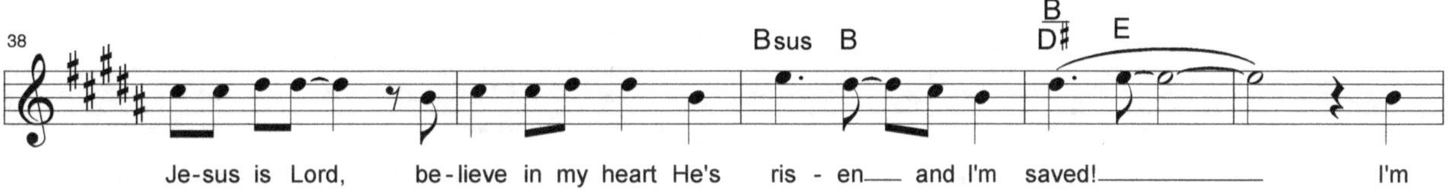

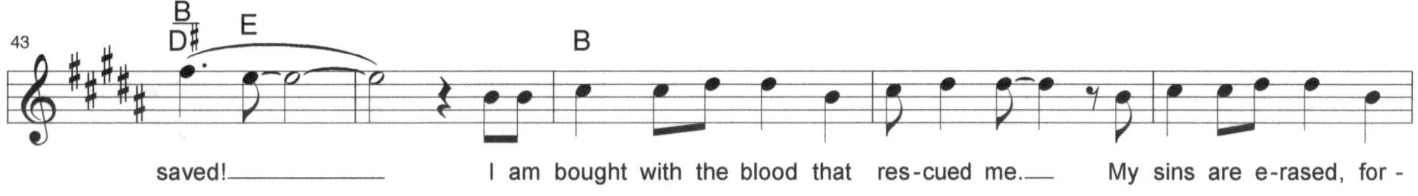

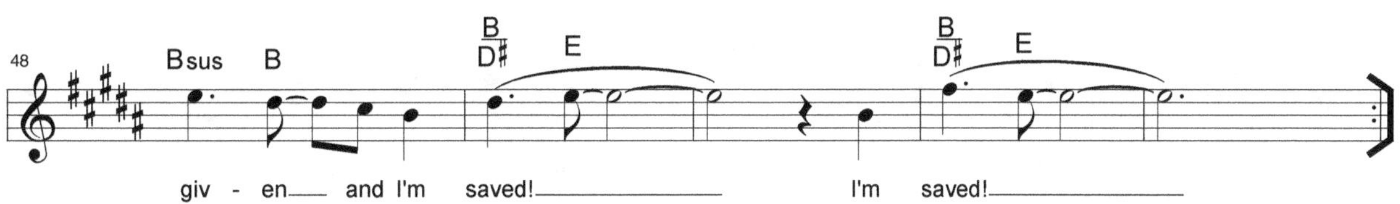

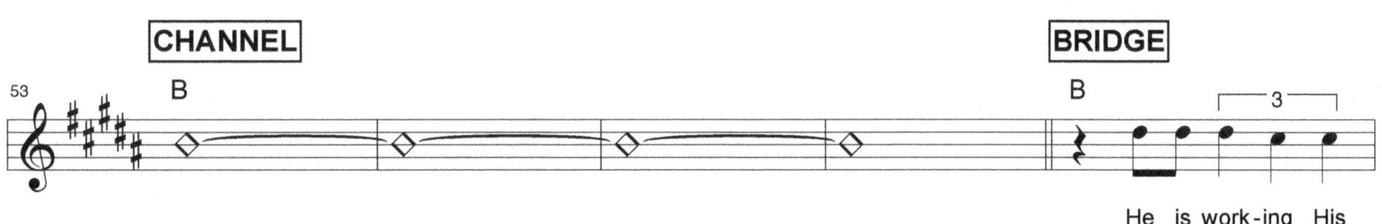

PAGE 3 - Saved

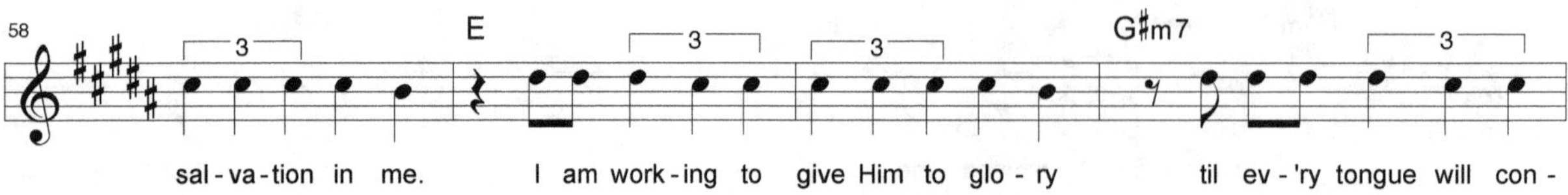
58
E
G♯m7
3
sal-va-tion in me. I am work-ing to give Him to glo-ry til ev-'ry tongue will con-

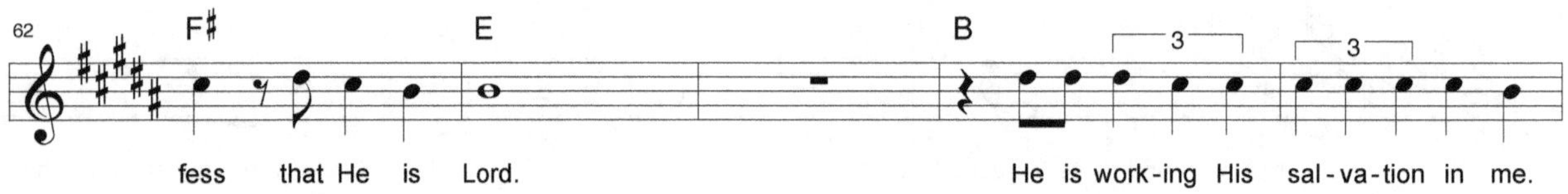
62
F♯
E
B
3
fess that He is Lord. He is work-ing His sal-va-tion in me.

67
E
G♯m7
F♯
3
I am work-ing to give Him to glo-ry til ev-'ry tongue will con-fess that He is

71
E
B
C♯m7
E
3
Lord. He is work-ing His sal-va-tion in me. I am work-ing to

76
F♯
G♯m7
F♯
E
3
give Him to glo-ry til ev-'ry tongue will con-fess that He is Lord. I de-

CHORUS
81
B
Bsus B
clare with my mouth that Je-sus is Lord, be-lieve in my heart He's ris-en and I'm

PAGE 4 - Saved

85
E
B
saved!
I'm saved!
I am bought with the blood that

90
Bsus B
E
res-cued me.
My sins are e-rased, for - giv - en and I'm saved!
I'm

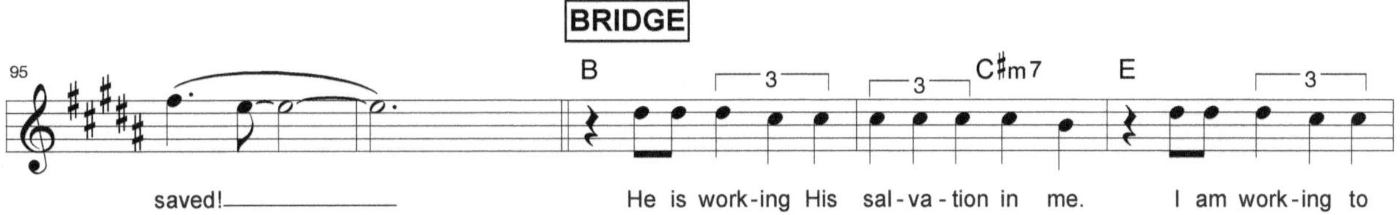
BRIDGE
95
B
C♯m7
E
3
saved!
He is work-ing His sal-va-tion in me.
I am work-ing to

100
F♯
G♯m7
F♯
E
3
give Him to glo-ry
til ev-'ry tongue will con-fess that He is Lord.

105
B
C♯m7
E
F♯
3
He is work-ing His sal - va - tion in me.
I am work-ing to give Him to glo - ry

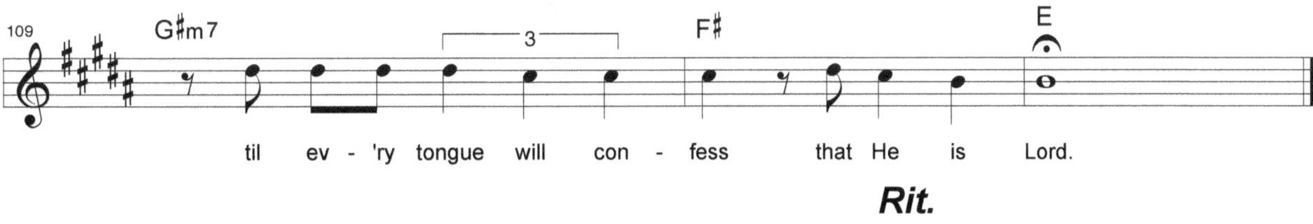
109
G♯m7
F♯
E
3
til ev - 'ry tongue will con - fess that He is Lord.
Rit.

Jesus My Savior (4:11)

(Micah Brooks/Jason Dyba)

Jesus My Savior is one of my favorite songs. I wrote it with my friend from Belmont University, Jason Dyba, at Lifeway headquarters in downtown Nashville, TN. I came to Jason with the melody that you hear in the song and Jason helped shaped the lyrics. He is a talented lyricist.

We began with the concept that the chorus needed to be simple and accessible while the verses could be more complex. Each verse describes an aspect of the character of Jesus and why His name is so great. We intentionally do not sing the name of Jesus until the chorus so that it lifts from the verses; not just with a melodic lift, but also in the power of the words. There is no name greater than the name of Jesus. No, not one!

Verse one speaks to the wonderful nature of his name. Everyone in heaven and on earth either does or will know it. The second verse is about the refuge nature of Jesus. He wants us all to come to a knowledge of Him and find rest. Verse three is about the grace and mercy of Jesus. Without the cross, we would not know His power and unsurpassable greatness. I love the triumphant words that death was beaten and slain. The cross was an agonizing defeat of darkness for light.

The bridge revisits each of the themes of the verses. Jesus' name is great and mighty. His reign is sovereign and everlasting. We can always run to Him. And His grace is the hope of Christ living deep inside of us now and forever.

May Jesus be your savior. May His mercy be everlasting and forget not soon all His benefits.

Lead Sheet
BPM = 80
Jesus My Savior
Micah Brooks Kennedy
and Jason Dyba
INTRO
C5 Csus C Am7 Am
Piano Intro Line
VERSE 1
F2 C Am7
I know the won-der - ful name all of the heav-ens ex-
F2 Am G
claim. It holds the pow - er to save. Won - der - ful is His name.
VERSE 2
C Am7
I know the re - fuge of life. He reigns in tow - er - ing might.
CHORUS
F2 Am G C G/B
All of my hope is in - side the re - fuge I've found in Christ. Je - sus, my
Am F C Am G C G/B Am F/A
Sav - ior, wor - thy, wor - thy! Mer - ci - ful Je - sus, my

PAGE 2 - Jesus My Savior

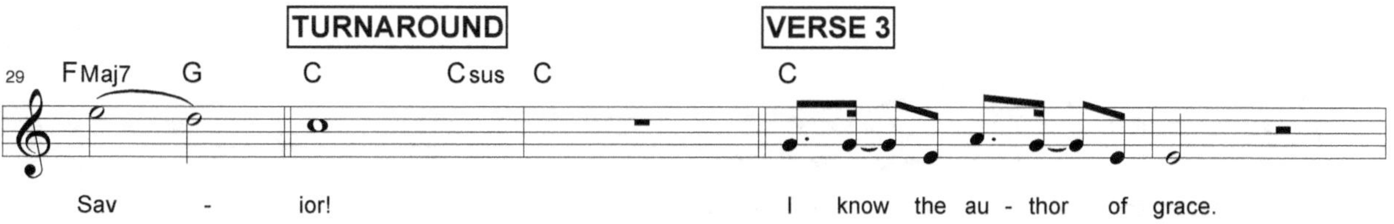

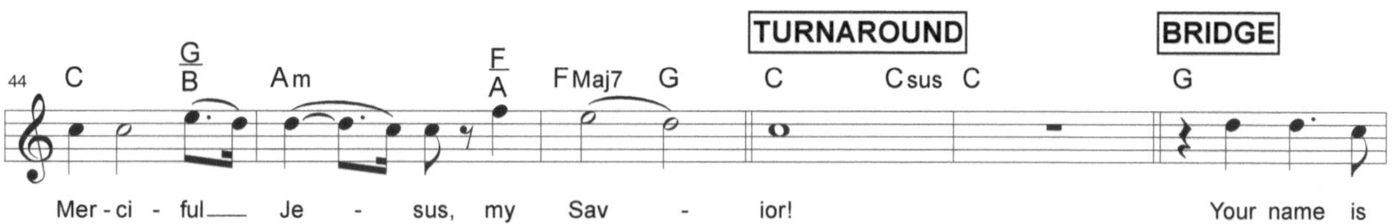

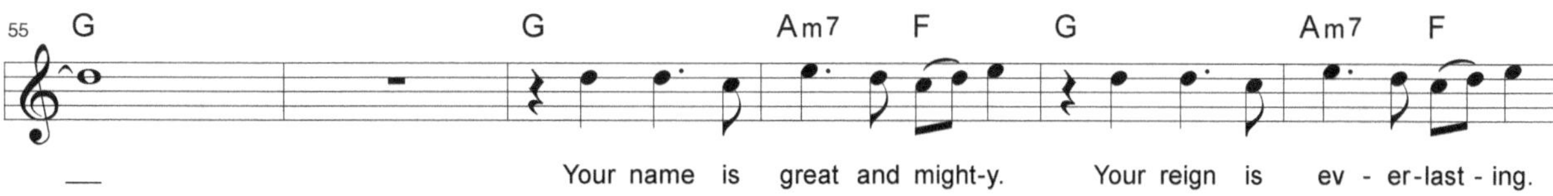

PAGE 3 - Jesus My Savior

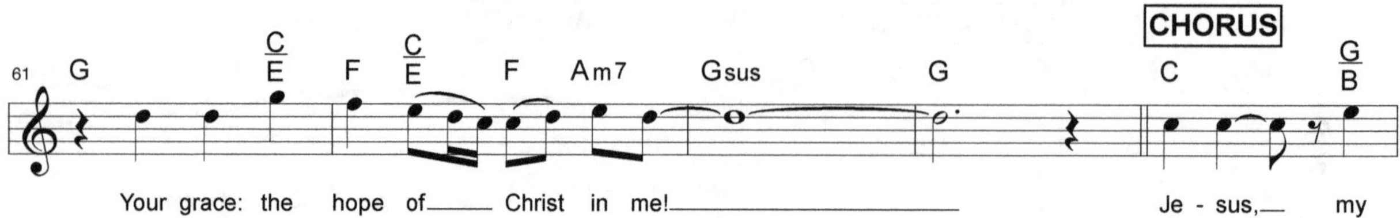

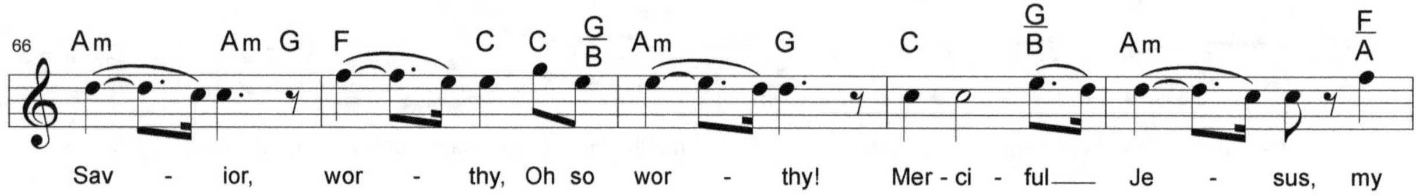

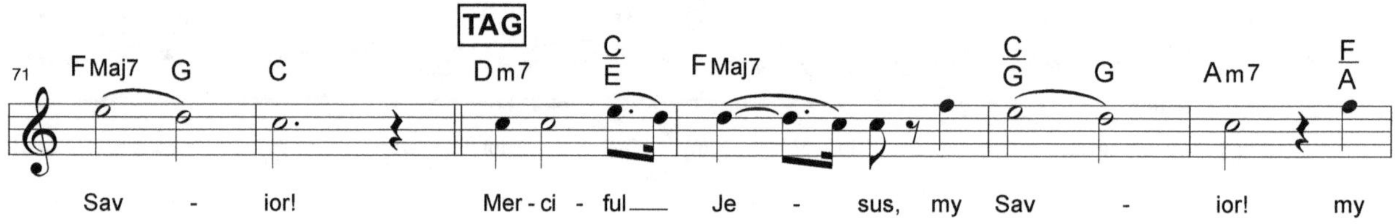

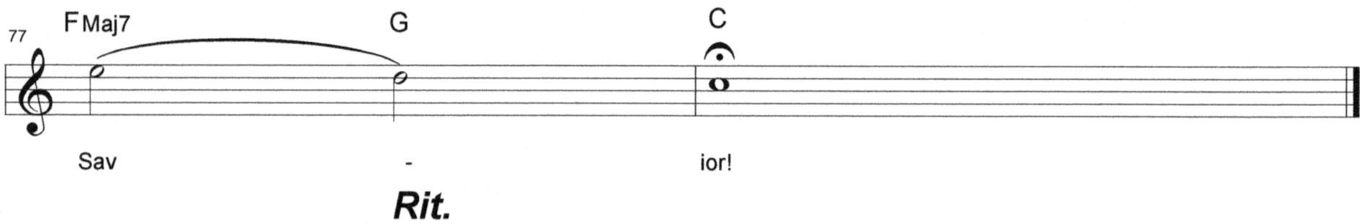

Here Comes The Lord (3:47)

(Micah Brooks/Jared Anderson)

I had the privilege of writing *Here Comes The Lord* with Jared Anderson. The day of writing was one of my favorite in my songwriting life. We wrote in the writer's room at Integrity Music in Franklin, TN.

Jared has become a friend and so we spent a few minutes catching about where our lives had led us recently before we began writing. In doing so, we realized that both of us were in seasons we would never have expected the Lord to bring us. I remember the line that Jared said speaking of his circumstance. He was talking about where his family was living for the summer and the opportunities that lay ahead for him and said, "But here comes the Lord to do it only as he can do". We then had the hook and idea for this song.

The hardest things in life usually come with skin attached. People affect us. The Lord, for whatever reason, leads us through difficult situations rather than around them. Even his own Son went to the cross, being so difficult that He sweated drops of blood. He even asked His Father to remove the cup from Him. We cannot expect anything different if God would treat his own Son this way.

In the chorus, we talk about understanding what God has already planned to bring us through and how he walks alongside us. He welcomes home the orphan; he rescues us; he uses challenges to refine us, but he always brings us back to him.

The name of this EP is *All Things New*. That line comes from the bridge of this song. The idea is that God is making all things new. He's making all things new again. We leak. We lose our trust in God but then he brings us back to him, time after time. God is able to do more than we could ever ask or imagine. Here comes the Lord to do what only he can do.

Here Comes The Lord

PAGE 2 - Here Comes The Lord

PAGE 3 - Here Comes The Lord

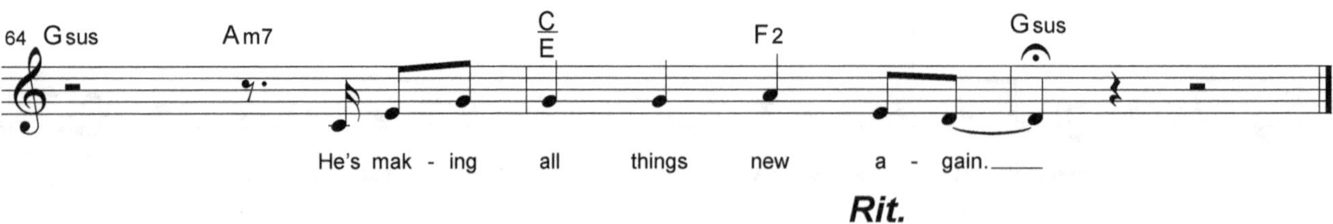

Rit.

Heal The Brokenhearted (4:16)

(Micah Brooks/Tony Wood)

Heal The Brokenhearted is the oldest song on the EP. I began writing it in 2011 when my mother-in-law was first diagnosed with a rare form of ovarian cancer. Amid that devastating news, I came across Psalm 147. Psalm 147:3 says that God is not only close to the brokenhearted, as it says so in Psalm 34:18, but also that he heals the brokenhearted.

The only one who can heal a broken heart is God. Many things can break it but God, our creator, is the only one who can restore it. In 2014, I had the chance to write with renowned lyricist Tony Wood. As we sat in the Word Entertainment writer's room in Franklin, TN, we began to talk about what was happening in our lives.

Tony asked me if I had any songs I had begun, but needed to finish. I went through a few ideas but nothing really hit home. I decided that I needed to be a bit more vulnerable and I brought forward the concept of *Heal The Brokenhearted*. Tony loved the hook and the premise behind it and so we got to work.

My favorite line in this tune is, "There's nothing shattered that You can't restore." If you think about a piece of glass that has shattered, even if you were able to glue everything back together, it would still be a fragmented window. However, when God restores something it is brand new. He makes all things new.

It was my privilege to play this song in front of my mother-in-law's casket at her funeral in 2016. She requested that I play a song that I had written and I knew this was the one she meant. We can trust that God will heal even the most broken of hearts. *Heal The Brokenhearted* is a victory chant as much as it is a prayer.

Heal The Brokenhearted

PAGE 2 - Heal The Brokenhearted

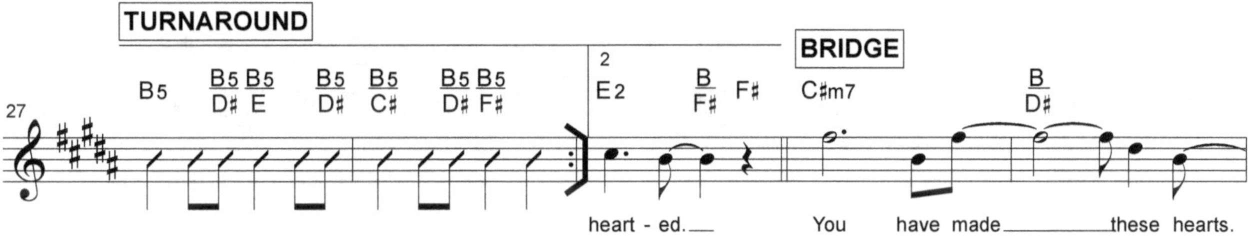

PAGE 3 - Heal The Brokenhearted

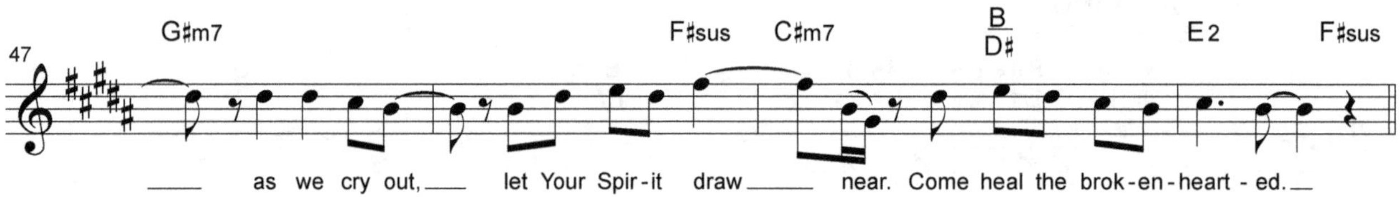

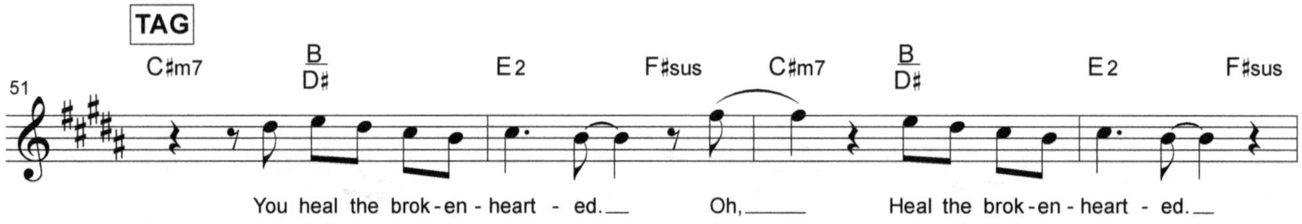

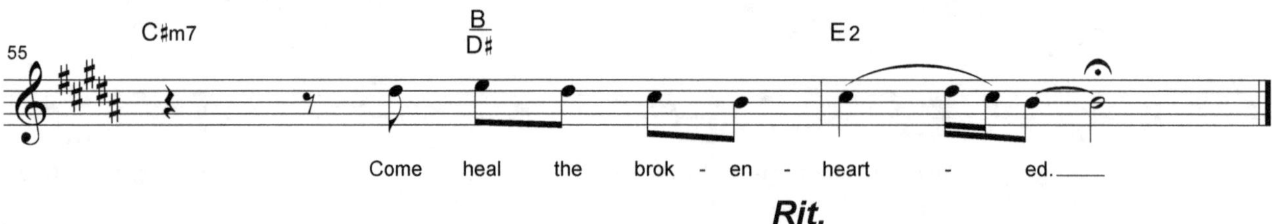

Love Has Overcome (4:12)

(Micah Brooks/Shelly E. Johnson)

Love Has Overcome is the Easter song of the record. It was a joy to write it with Shelly E. Johnson. We both attended Belmont University together, having mutual friends, but had never written together. Shelly has an incredible heart for worship leading and it shows in her writing style.

When you read the final days of Jesus' life across all four of the gospels you realize how focused Jesus' determination had to be to achieve His goal. His being fully God, yet fully man made these days agonizing. Shelly and I loved the line that begins this song by saying, "Hear the sound of glory rising." The idea is like a trumpet announcing the entrance of a great king. Our praises, when amassed together, are a wonderful and frightful sound. God's people, using the power that raised Jesus from the dead, is no force with which to be reckoned.

The chorus is an important reminder that it was Jesus' precious love that overcame sin and the grave. The Bible says that He became a curse for us. It wasn't that He entertained the curse, but that He became the curse. When we sing of His great love, and the power that helped Him overcome, we are singing about the dreadful curse that we placed upon Him. The glorious reveal is that He is triumphant, removing the curse forever! He is risen indeed!

I love the lift of the bridge, "Jesus, Jesus there is none but Jesus." Jesus said that no one can come to the Father except through Him. He is the gatekeeper where there had been no open door before. We now have access to the Father in a way that only Jesus and the angels knew.

I love the opportunity of this song on Easter Sunday. When we know what has been overcome and why it matters today, we can sing it with all of our hearts. We are far better off because of Jesus' shed blood today than even yesterday. It's amazing that His mercies are made new each and every morning. Praise God!

Love Has Overcome

Lead Sheet
BPM = 71

Micah Brooks Kennedy
and Shelly E. Johnson

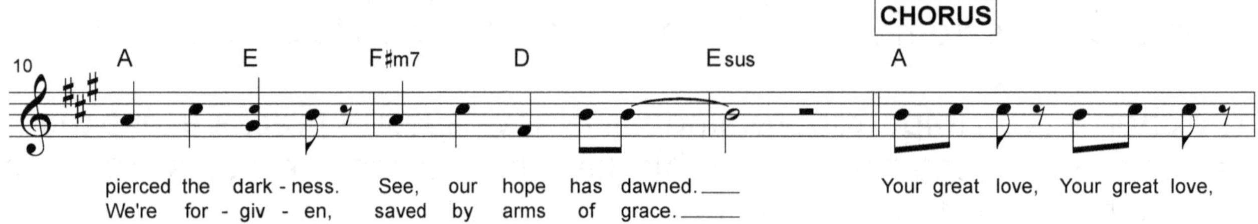

Your great love has o - ver - come. God has won. Death un - done. Praise be to the Ris - en Son. Your great love has

PAGE 2 - Love Has Overcome

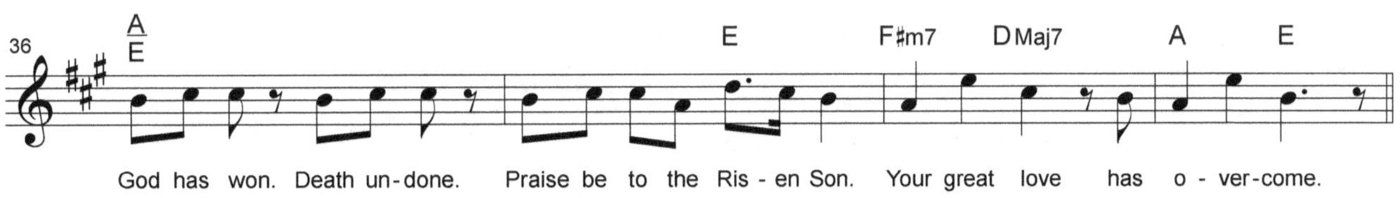

PAGE 3 - Love Has Overcome

And he who was seated on the throne said,
"Behold, I am making all things new."
-Revelation 21:5

BPM=114

I V C V C B C Tag

All To Your Name (1 of 2)

Micah Brooks Kennedy, Corey Voss

INTRO

| G | G | G/B | G/B | C | C | G C6/G^ **| C6/G |**

VERSE

```
G
I was lost but now I'm found
G/B
I was broken I was bound
    C                              | G  C6/G^  | C6/G |
But then Your mercy set this sinner free
G
You are making all things new
     G/B
Your morning light is breaking through
     C                               | G | G |
Your perfect love has made me come alive
```

CHORUS

```
  G                   Gsus  G
I raise my hands up to the sky
   G                     Gsus  G
To praise the name of Jesus Christ
    Em7                 C2           | G  C6/G^  | C6/G |
The one who taught my heart to rise in worship
  G         Gsus  G
I give my life to magnify
    G                    Gsus  G
All to Your name Lord Jesus Christ
      Em7           C2         | G | G |
Who was and is and is to come I worship
```

VERSE

```
G
This great hope I hold inside
G/B
I won't bury I won't hide
     C                             | G  C6/G^  | C6/G |
Your goodness calling me to tell the world
G
You are coming back again
     G/B
With eyes like fire breath like wind
     C                               | G | G |
Your every word is faithful it is true
```

All To Your Name (2 of 2)

CHORUS

```
   G                    Gsus   G
I raise my hands up to the sky
    G                     Gsus  G
To praise the name of Jesus Christ
     Em7                   C2           | G  C6/G^  | C6/G |
The one who taught my heart to rise in worship
  G               Gsus  G
I give my life to magnify
    G                     Gsus  G
All to Your name Lord Jesus Christ
     Em7              C2         | G | G |
Who was and is and is to come I worship
```

BRIDGE

```
           CMaj9              Dsus
All the saints all hands raised
         CMaj9/E      Dsus/F#
Every praise all to Your name
         CMaj9       Dsus
Jesus Christ glorified
          Em7          Dsus/F#
Every praise all to Your name
           CMaj9              Dsus
All the saints all hands raised
          CMaj9/E     Dsus/F#
Every praise all to Your name
         CMaj9       Dsus
Jesus Christ glorified
          Em7          Dsus/F#  |  Dsus/F#  |
Every praise all to Your name
```

CHORUS

```
   G
I raise my hands up to the sky
    G
To praise the name of Jesus Christ
     Em7                   C2           | G | G (Hits on "3" "and") |
The one who taught my heart to rise in worship
  G               Gsus  G
I give my life to magnify
    G                    Gsus  G
All to Your name Lord Jesus Christ
     Em7              C2         | G | G |
Who was and is and is to come I worship
     Em7              C2         | G | G |
Who was and is and is to come I worship
     Em7◇             C2◇          G◇
Who was and is and is to come I worship
```

BPM=130 I ½C T V C V C Ch B C B

Saved (1 of 2)

Micah Brooks Kennedy, Kirk Kirkland

INTRO
```
        | B | B | B | B |
```

CHORUS
```
           B
I declare with my mouth that Jesus is Lord
   B                        Bsus  B          B/D#  E  |  E  |  B/D#  E  |  E◇  |
Believe in my heart He's ris - en and I'm saved            I'm saved
```

TURNAROUND
```
| B | B | B | Bsus B | B/D# E | E | B/D# E | E |
```

VERSE
```
B         C#m           F#
With my heart I do believe
G#m      F#                 E
With my mouth I must confess
B       C#m                   F#
Jesus' blood has ransomed me
G#m       F#                 E
Now my soul has found it's rest
```

CHORUS
```
           B
I declare with my mouth that Jesus is Lord
   B                        Bsus  B          B/D#  E  |  E  |  B/D#  E  |  E  |
Believe in my heart He's ris - en and I'm saved            I'm saved
      B
I am bought with the blood that rescued me
    B                    Bsus  B          B/D#  E  |  E  |  B/D#  E  |  E  |
My sins are erased forgiv  -  en and I'm saved            I'm saved
```

VERSE
```
B            C#m               F#
Share the joy of this good news
G#m    F#            E
Our belief is without shame
B      C#m                   F#
Jesus died that we might choose
G#m       F#                 E
To make known his saving grace
```

Repeat Chorus

Saved (2 of 2)

```
CHANNEL
      | B◇^  | B◇^  | B◇^  | B◇  |

BRIDGE
      B
      He is working His salvation in me
      E
      I am working to give Him the glory
      G#m                       F#          | E | E |
      'Til every tongue will confess that He is Lord
      B
      He is working His salvation in me
      E
      I am working to give Him the glory
      G#m                       F#          | E | E |
      'Til every tongue will confess that He is Lord
      B                           C#m
      He is working His salvation in me
      E                             F#
      I am working to give Him the glory
      G#m                       F#          | E | E |
      'Til every tongue will confess that He is Lord

CHORUS
          B
      I declare with my mouth that Jesus is Lord
         B                     Bsus  B          E | E | E | E |
      Believe in my heart He's ris - en and I'm saved   I'm saved
           B
      I am bought with the blood that rescued me
         B                   Bsus  B          E | E | E | E |
      My sins are erased forgiv  -  en and I'm saved   I'm saved

BRIDGE
      B                           C#m
      He is working His salvation in me
      E                             F#
      I am working to give Him the glory
      G#m                       F#          | E | E |
      'Til every tongue will confess that He is Lord
      B                           C#m
      He is working His salvation in me
      E                             F#
      I am working to give Him the glory
      G#m                       F#            E2◇
      'Til every tongue will confess that He is Lord
                                  Rit.
```

BPM=80 I V V C V C B C Tag

Jesus My Savior (1 of 2)

Micah Brooks Kennedy, Jason Dyba

INTRO

```
| C5 Csus | C | Am7 | Am | F2 | F2 |
```

VERSE

```
C
I know the wonderful name
Am7
All of the heavens exclaim
F2
It holds the power to save
           Am   G
Wonderful is His name
```

VERSE

```
C
I know the refuge of life
Am7
He reigns in towering might
F2
All of my hope is inside
               Am      G
The refuge I've found in Christ
```

CHORUS

```
C     G/B  Am
Jesus my   savior
F     C   Am   G
Worthy    worthy
C     G/B  Am   F/A  FMaj7  G  | C Csus | C |
Merciful   Jesus my  sa      -    vior
```

VERSE

```
C
I know the author of grace
Am7
Dying He hung in my place
F2
Death He has beaten and slain
        Am     G
This is amazing grace
```

Jesus My Savior (2 of 2)

CHORUS

```
C      G/B  Am
Jesus my   savior
F     C   Am    G
Worthy   worthy
C      G/B  Am     F/A   FMaj7  G  |  C  Csus  |  C  |
Merciful     Jesus  my    sa     -       vior
```

BRIDGE

```
G               Am         F
Your name is great and mighty
G              Am  F
Your reign is everlasting
G            C/E  F         Am      G
Your grace the   hope of Christ in me
G               Am         F
Your name is great and mighty
G              Am  F
Your reign is everlasting
G            C/E  F     C/E  F     Am  |  G  |  G  |
Your grace the   hope of    Christ in       me
```

CHORUS

```
C      G/B  Am
Jesus my   savior
F     C   Am    G
Worthy   worthy
C      G/B  Am     F/A   FMaj7  G  |  C  |
Merciful     Jesus  my    sa     -       vior
```

TAG

```
Dm   C/E  FMaj7      C/G  G   |  Am  |
Merciful   Jesus  my   sa    -    vior
F/A  FMaj7◇  G◇  |  C◇
My   sa        -     vior
                Rit.
```

BPM=74 I V C V C B C CTag BTag

Here Comes The Lord (1 of 2)

Micah Brooks Kennedy, Jared Anderson

INTRO
```
| Am7  C  |  F2  G  |  Am7  C  |  F2  G  |
```

VERSE
```
Am7          C            F2
My Father's full of compassion
G              Am7  C         |  F2  G  |
He is not afraid   He is not afraid
Am7             C             F2
And when His children are hurting
   G                 Am7     C              |  F2  G  |
He never hides his face      never hides His face
```

CHORUS
```
(G)                 C        Gsus
Here comes the Lord to gather up the broken
   Am7                                F2
To welcome home the orphan to rescue us
     Gsus         C          Gsus
Here comes the Lord with fire for refining
   Am7                         F2             |  F2(#4)◇  |
In heaven's perfect timing He brings us back
```

VERSE
```
Am7          C                F2
My Father's endlessly faithful
    G                Am7  C           |  F2  G  |
He's everything I need  everything I need
Am7            C                F2
The more I taste the more I hunger
   G               Am7  C          |  F2  G  |
For all He has for me     All He has for me
```

CHORUS
```
(G)                 C        Gsus
Here comes the Lord to gather up the broken
   Am7                                F2
To welcome home the orphan to rescue us
     Gsus         C          Gsus
Here comes the Lord with fire for refining
   Am7                         F
In heaven's perfect timing He brings us back
```

Here Comes The Lord (2 of 2)

```
BRIDGE
                    C/E       F2  |  G  Am7  |
      He's making all things new
                    C/E       F2  |  G  |
      He's making all things new   again
             C/E       F2  |  G  Am7  |
      He's making all things new
                    C/E       F2  |  G  |
      He's making all things new   again

CHORUS
      (G)                 C       Gsus
      Here comes the Lord to gather up the broken
         Am7                              F2
      To welcome home the orphan to rescue us
           Gsus        C          Gsus
      Here comes the Lord with fire for refining
         Am7                             F
      In heaven's perfect timing He brings us back

CHORUS TAG
           G              C  |  Gsus  |
      Here comes the Lord
                         Am7    F2
      Here comes the Lord to rescue us
           G              C  |  Gsus  |
      Here comes the Lord
                         Am7    F2           |  F2(#4)◇  |
      Here comes the Lord to bring us back

BRIDGE TAG
                    C/E       F2  |  G  Am7  |
      He's making all things new
                    C/E       F2    G◇
      He's making all things new again
                                  Rit.
```

BPM=75

I V C T V C B C Tag

Heal The Brokenhearted (1 of 2)

Micah Brooks Kennedy, Tony Wood

INTRO

```
| B  E2  | C#m  F#sus  | B  E2  | C#m  F#sus  |
```

VERSE

```
B     E2  | C#m        F#sus       B
We come             and pour out our pain
(B)  E2  | C#m   F#sus       G#m7
Undone            by sorrow and shame
(G#m7)  E2  | C#m  F#sus          G#m7
Each one                  wounded and bruised
(G#m7)  E2  | C#m  F#sus
By life                   we cry
```

CHORUS

```
B                                 F#/A#  G#m7
Almighty God there's no power like Yours
(G#m7)                                     F#  C#m7
There's nothing shattered that You can't restore
(C#m7)  B/D#          | E2  F#sus  |
Come     heal the brokenhearted
B                                   F#/A#  G#m7
We come in faith Jesus we come in tears
(G#m7)                       F#     C#m7
As we cry out let Your Spirit draw near
(C#m7)  B/D#          | E2  E2  F#sus  |
Come     heal the brokenhearted
C#m7     B/D#         | E2  F#sus  |
Come     heal the brokenhearted
```

TURNAROUND

```
| B  E2  | C#m  F#sus  |
```

VERSE

```
B     E2  | C#m        F#sus      B
Be close            in the places we grieve
(B)  E2  | C#m   F#sus       G#m7
Speak hope  in our moment of need
(G#m7)  E2  | C#m  F#sus        G#m7
We know             Your presence is here
(G#m7)  E2  | C#m  F#sus
With faith              we say
```

Heal The Brokenhearted (2 of 2)

CHORUS

B   F#/A# G#m7
Almighty God there's no power like Yours
(G#m7)   F# C#m7
There's nothing shattered that You can't restore
(C#m7) B/D# | E2 F#sus |
Come   heal the brokenhearted
B   F#/A# G#m7
We come in faith Jesus we come in tears
(G#m7)   F#   C#m7
As we cry out let Your Spirit draw near
(C#m7) B/D# | E2 E2 F#sus |
Come   heal the brokenhearted
C#m7   B/D# | E2 F#sus |
Come   heal the brokenhearted

BRIDGE

C#m7   B/D#   E2   F#
You have made these hearts You can heal the brokenhearted
C#m7   B/D#   E2   C#m7 | C#m7◊ |
You have made these hearts You can heal the brokenhearted

CHORUS

B   F#/A# G#m7
Almighty God there's no power like Yours
(G#m7)   F# C#m7
There's nothing shattered that You can't restore
(C#m7) B/D# | E2 F#sus |
Come   heal the brokenhearted
B   F#/A# G#m7
We come in faith Jesus we come in tears
(G#m7)   F#   C#m7
As we cry out let Your Spirit draw near
(C#m7) B/D# | E2 E2 F#sus |
Come   heal the brokenhearted
C#m7   B/D# | E2 E2 F#sus |
You   heal the brokenhearted
C#m7   B/D# | E2 E2 F#sus |
Oh   Heal the brokenhearted
C#m7   B/D# | E2◊
Come   heal the brokenhearted
Rit.

BPM=71

IVCTVCBCCB

Love Has Overcome (1 of 2)

Micah Brooks Kennedy, Shelly E. Johnson

```
INTRO
        | F#m7  D2  |  A  E  | F#m7  D2  |  Esus  E  |

VERSE
        F#m7    D2        A     E
        Hear the sound of glory rising
        F#m7  D2      |  Esus  E  |
        Join in freedom's song
        F#m7    D2         A        E
        Heaven's light has pierced the darkness
        F#m7  D2      |  Esus  |
        See our hope has dawned

CHORUS
        A                                                   Asus  A
        Your great love Your great love Your great love has overcome
        A/E                                           A/E  E
        God has won death undone praise be to the risen Son
        F#m7       DMaj7    A    E
        Your great love has overcome
        F#m7       DMaj7    A    E
        Your great love has overcome

TURNAROUND
        | F#m7  D2  |  A  E  |

VERSE
        F#m7   D2       A          E
        Heaven wept as Christ was broken
        F#m7  D2     |  Esus  E  |
        Perfect love was slain
        F#m7   D2            A        E
        Sin was vanquished we're forgiven
        F#m7    D2   |  Esus  E  |
        Saved by arms of grace

CHORUS
        A                                                   Asus  A
        Your great love Your great love Your great love has overcome
        A/E                                           A/E  E
        God has won death undone praise be to the risen Son
        F#m7       DMaj7    A    E
        Your great love has overcome
        F#m7       DMaj7    A    E
        Your great love has overcome
```

Love Has Overcome (2 of 2)

BRIDGE

D2 F#m7 E
Jesus Jesus there is none but Jesus
D2 F#m7 E
Savior Savior You alone are Savior
D2 F#m7 E
Jesus Jesus there is none but Jesus
D2 F#m7 E | D2 | D2 |
Savior Savior You alone are Savior

CHORUS

A Asus A
Your great love Your great love Your great love has overcome
A/E A/E E
God has won death undone praise be to the risen Son
F#m7 DMaj7 A E
Your great love has overcome

CHORUS

A Bm A
Your great love Your great love Your great love has overcome
A/E A/E E
God has won death undone praise be to the risen Son
F#m7 DMaj7 A E
Your great love has overcome
F#m7 DMaj7 $\frac{2}{4}$A | $\frac{4}{4}$E(Stop on Beat "4") **|**
Your great love has overcome

BRIDGE

DMaj7 F#m7 E
Jesus Jesus there is none but Jesus
DMaj7 F#m7 E
Savior Savior You alone are Savior
DMaj7 F#m7 E
Jesus Jesus there is none but Jesus
DMaj7 F#m7 E | D2◇
Savior Savior You alone are Savior

Connect With Micah Brooks

Signup for Micah Brooks emails to stay up to date

Subscribe to the Micah Brooks Company "Stay Connected" email list for the latest music and book releases. This email list is always free and intended to deliver high value content to your inbox. Visit the link below to signup.

www.micahbrooks.com/signup

Contact Micah

Email Micah Brooks at micahbrooks.com/contact. I want to know who you are. It's my privilege to respond to your emails personally. Please feel free to connect.

Please share this songbook with your friends

If you would like to share your thanks for this book, the best thing you can do is to tell a friend about Micah Brooks: "All Things New EP Songbook" or buy them a copy. You can also show your appreciation for this book by leaving a review.

More About Micah Brooks Company

For more about Micah Brooks Company, including books, CDs, mp3s, Micah Brooks Design Co., online store, blogs, devotions, speaking, and performing dates go to:

www.micahbrooks.com

Micah and Rochelle: Better Together for the Kingdom of God

My wife, Rochelle, and I share a ministry together at micahandrochelle.com. We would be honored to have you come to our website. You will find a membership site and articles about family, parenting, women-only and men-only sections and more. Also, listen to our podcast, Better Together Podcast: A Christian Marriage and Family Show available on iTunes. For more information visit:

www.micahandrochelle.com

Follow Micah Brooks:

Facebook: @micahbrooksofficial
Twitter: @micahbrooksco
LinkedIn: Micah Brooks
Instagram: @micahbrooksco

www.ingramcontent.com/pod-product-compliance
Lightning Source LLC
LaVergne TN
LVHW081424110826
845149LV00010B/1866
* 9 7 8 0 9 9 9 6 9 3 7 0 4 *